SHARE~A~BOOK CLUB

DONATED BY

Gregory & Sally Connell

IN MEMORY OF

Jessie Green

J. D. BANCROFT   ~   1994

Sky Gardens

Rooftops, Balconies, and Terraces

Signe Nielsen

Sky Gardens

Rooftops, Balconies, and Terraces

Signe Nielsen

Schiffer Publishing Ltd

4880 Lower Valley Road, Atglen, PA 19310 USA

Dedication

To my daughter, Marina, whose words bring me endless joy and
to my husband, Roi, whose keen sensibilities make me see more clearly.

Library of Congress Cataloging-in-Publication Data

Nielsen, Signe.
    Sky gardens: rooftops, balconies, and terraces/by Signe
Nielsen.
      p. cm.
    ISBN 0-7643-2004-1
1. Roof gardening. 2. Balcony gardening. 3. Patio gardening. I. Title
SB419.5.N45 2004
635.9'671—dc22

                        2003023076

Designed by John P. Cheek
Cover Design by Bruce Waters
Type set in Verdana/Zurich BT

ISBN: 0-7643-2004-1
Printed in China

Published by Schiffer Publishing Ltd.
4880 Lower Valley Road
Atglen, PA 19310
Phone: (610) 593-1777; Fax: (610) 593-2002
E-mail: Info@schifferbooks.com

For the largest selection of fine reference books
on this and related subjects, please visit our
web site at **www.schifferbooks.com**
We are always looking for people to write
books on new and related subjects. If you have
an idea for a book please contact us at the
above address.

This book may be purchased from the pub-
lisher.
Include $3.95 for shipping.
Please try your bookstore first.
You may write for a free catalog.

In Europe, Schiffer books are distributed by
Bushwood Books
6 Marksbury Ave.
Kew Gardens
Surrey TW9 4JF England
Phone: 44 (0) 20 8392-8585;
Fax: 44 (0) 20 8392-9876
E-mail: info@bushwoodbooks.co.uk
Free postage in the U.K., Europe; air mail at
cost.

Contents

Acknowledgments

This book has given me the opportunity to compile my work and photographs that span more than thirty years. Many of the designs would not have been accomplished without the invaluable help and humor of Dudley Mason and our talented gardeners, Jeff Mendoza, Peter Diffly, and Bill Meyerson. Some of the more recent examples have been done in collaboration with my extraordinary partner, Kim Mathews and the creative staff of Mathews Nielsen Landscape Architects PC. Still other examples are from my travels and are offered to expand the spectrum of possibilities. Many of the best photographs have been taken by our firm's photographers, James Morse and Max Donoso Saint. I wish to thank them all for their dedication and hard work. May we each continue to strive for beauty through our creative endeavors.

Introduction

Your sky garden is a special addition to your living environment. Converting a terrace or rooftop into a private haven high above the world below offers a welcome chance to linger outdoors in solitude or with friends. Your new-found space enlarges a living area, provides a safe place to play, a quiet corner to read, and a sheltered spot for entertaining. It may evoke the sense of boundless space or offer inward-looking shelter.

The intent of this book is to inspire you to transform an underused outdoor space into a sanctuary that is a reflection of your taste, lifestyle, time, and budget. Your garden needs to be comfortable and convenient as well as beautiful and inviting. The spectrum of examples offered will help encourage your own ideas on ways to adapt design solutions to suit your particular needs and conditions.

Designing the terrace or rooftop garden begins by understanding what you have and what you want. Examine the opportunities that accompany your outdoor space – sun, shade, breezes, and views. Evaluate the constraints – lack of privacy, a blank wall, an awkward shape. Chapter One contains a variety of hidden treasures from which to select ideas that best exemplify your vision.

Once you have decided on a general theme, the next step is to consider the boundaries of your space. Chapter Two illustrates various alternatives to using perimeter elements to delineate the vertical and overhead framework of your space. Railings, fences, and screens become invitations to create privacy, open up views, or subdivide a larger area while arbors and sun shades define protected outdoor rooms.

The floor of your garden is critical to its character. In Chapter Three you will find an array of options for paving, decks, and even level changes to enhance the sky garden and unite its components into a cohesive whole.

Adding vegetation to your garden requires containers to hold the soil and plants. Chapter Four presents a plethora of ideas from small pots to large planters and recessed trays to achieve the landscape of your fantasy. Chapter Five helps you select planting arrangements tailored to your location, container sizes, and garden theme.

Locating places to read, dine, or relax needs to be considered in relation to the ambience you wish to create. Comfort, views, shade, and intimacy are some of the qualities that foster prolonged enjoyment. Chapter Six offers choices and considerations for furnishing the sky garden.

Bring your garden to life at night by adding lighting. Chapter Seven displays some of the techniques available to illuminate surfaces or highlight featured elements. The finishing touches can be found in Chapter Eight where examples of sculpture, fountains, and unique comforts help make your sanctuary distinctly your own.

Whether your desire is for an outdoor room that exhibits the qualities of permanence and stability or a garden that expresses seasonal change and ephemeral nature, this book will stimulate your imagination to envision the endless possibilities of beautiful landscapes in the sky.

Starting Out

Roof gardens, terraces, and balconies are artificial environments yet they enable the urban dweller to create a meaningful relationship among a home, its residents, and nature.

Design of a sky garden entails both problem-solving and imagination to address three basic factors: natural conditions of climate, structural elements of the architecture, and your needs and preferences.

The transition from inside to outside is critically important. This is the occasion to extend your interior living space outwards and to invite enjoyment of your private exterior refuge.

10

High above the street, terraces, balconies, and roof gardens offer the extraordinary possibility of blurring the distinction between the ground and the sky.

Exploit your surroundings. Use surfaces such as walls, floors, and level changes to define a personal sanctuary that suits your lifestyle.

11

A Sense of Place

There are limitless ways to create a special place. If your terrace has a dramatic vista, consider framing a skyline landmark. Borrowing a distant view of the cityscape is a unique opportunity of urban gardens.

Creating an enticing foreground is an effective technique to distract from an uninteresting background. The arbor beckons the visitor to explore the outdoors and provides an overhead transition from the ceiling to the sky.

12

In hot climates an arbor offers welcome shade as well as a sense of enclosure converting a corridor into a usable exterior room.

13

14

Spiral stairs fit into tight corners affording access to a forgotten place. Tall bamboo and a checker-board pattern of moss and polished stones transform the space into a peaceful refuge. *Photo by Max Donoso Saint.*

Once outside, the design should greet the visitor with commodious comforts, secret passages, and secluded corners. *Photo by James Morse.*

A garden in the sky is a way to celebrate daily pleasures. Take advantage of large spaces and expansive views for alfresco entertaining.

15

Design Techniques

Long narrow terraces can be made more interesting by staggering the placement of geometric planters. The square shapes are a strong form that is repeated by the use of equally robust architectural plantings.

Rectangular, recessed plant beds arranged in a maze-like layout create a dynamic pattern and choreograph movement through the gravel paths.

A large square roof lacks orientation or focus. The angular plant bed generates a sense of direction and contrasts with the curved roof. Alternating bands of colored pavers further enhance the feeling of movement.

17

A broad terrace has sufficient width to accommodate a curvilinear planting bed that undulates like a wave along the building wall.

Inserting a curved form into a rectilinear space announces a prominent viewing spot. The composition is enriched by subtle diagonal shifts in the decking and wood railing.

19

Soft curves of a linear planter and circular freestanding planters are positioned to gracefully terminate a terrace thus avoiding a dead end corner.

Diagonally placed terra cotta urns interlock arched and rectangular architectural forms to create a dynamic composition.

Juxtaposition of contrasting materials can produce a spirited combination even in a small space.

20

A well-designed terrace offers a variety of experiences. Planters, lattice panels, and even a chimney can be used to subdivide space and form a sequence of rooms.

By accentuating the linear narrow passage with a long line of low planting, movement as well as the eye, are directed to the end where a taller shrub announces a change in direction.

21

A staggered arrangement of planters suggests diagonal movement around the building corner and directs the visitor toward the principal gathering area of the terrace. *Photo by James Morse.*

Below:
A balanced composition of paired forms is an example of a symmetrical layout. Symmetry in landscape design is most often associated with a formal garden.

Visual equilibrium on a smaller scale can be effective in creating a foreground focal point juxtaposed with an asymmetrically framed view of a landmark spire in the distance. *Photo by Max Donoso Saint.*

In lieu of rigid symmetry, a composition of classical shapes uses a central focal feature as its organizing device.

Asymmetrical planting beds with a loose planting arrangement are more informal in feeling. Repetition of forms and plants helps avoid visual confusion when the layout is irregular. *Photo by Max Donoso Saint.*

24

25

Proportion and scale are both relative terms used to describe a relationship among elements. Selection of containers, plantings, and furnishings is dependent on the size and weight limits of a sky garden. The goal is to achieve a dialogue between hard and soft materials that look well together. *Photo by James Morse.*

Frames are intended to define the boundaries of a space. A clipped hedge reinforces the simple geometry of the furniture and metal planter resulting in a clean-edged design.

On larger roof terraces framing devices may alternate between solid enclosures of plants or walls and more visually transparent fences. Coordinate your perimeter treatments to open up vistas or block undesirable winds.

26

Accents are special features that draw attention because of their placement or inherent beauty. Locate focal points to maximize their ability to be appreciated from interior rooms or as outdoor destinations.

27

28

Design needs to be a reflection of your taste. Examine your indoor surroundings for clues about your preferences. A classical style has a timeless elegance that uses strong architectural forms paired with soft plant shapes. *Photo by James Morse.*

An Asian style garden uses balance rather than symmetry to create a composition. Natural materials of rock, sand, water, and plants are organized in geometrical shapes composed to create a picture framed by a bamboo screen.

A modern garden relies on bold geometry, simple materials, and an asymmetrical layout. Each planter contains only one type of plant to reinforce the purity of form. *Photo by James Morse.*

A modern garden is also a place to experiment with materials. Innovations in lightweight concrete and recycled materials are used for the hardscape elements while the plant palette masses bamboo and grasses that are distinctly soft and supple. *Photo by Max Donoso Saint.*

Minimalism refines a space to sculptural proportions. Simplicity of elements creates an uncluttered environment that is soothing and peaceful. The minimalist style encourages materials that reveal their essential character and function. Industrial fiberglass decking, unpainted galvanized metal, and coarse volcanic rocks are combined with a few plant species to form a distinctive oasis.

This Mediterranean style terrace illustrates the beauty of regional design. Local architecture and material availability help simplify choices and ensure compatibility between the outdoors and its geographic environment. Choosing plants that are native to your climate are more likely to survive without expensive maintenance.

Outdoor spaces in hot, humid regions need protection from sun and rain. Lush plants and sculptural forms complement architectural overhangs and shade structures.

Gardens of the northwest are influenced by climate and Asian traditions. This simple terrace relies on borrowed scenery to create an inviting, weather-protected vantage point.

Infused by a variety of stylistic traditions, gardens of the southeast region use an eclectic mix of materials and seasonally expressive plantings to create a shady, restful retreat.

The northeast and midwest are subject to extremes of temperature and wind. Evergreen and deciduous plant combinations offer year-round interest to be enjoyed from inside or outside.

Creating the feel of a country garden on a terrace does not require much space. Weathered wood, an old wheelbarrow and free-flowing plants engender charming, unpretentious comfort.

36

A secret garden has a mysterious quality that inspires a journey to explore its hidden corners and verdant passages.

Misty colors, privacy, and a whimsical table lend a romantic air to this terrace. Tall shrubs block the world outside making a secluded haven infused with scented flowers. *Photo by James Morse.*

Enjoying the outdoors needs little more than comfortable chaise lounges, a side table, and thoughtful placement. A vine-covered trellis blocks north winds while the west is left open to watch glorious sunsets. *Photo by James Morse.*

Entertaining friends in all seasons is a certainty if you combine a greenhouse addition with an outdoor terrace. The glass-enclosed room provides direct access to the kitchen and the generously sized door allows furniture to be brought in or out.

A wild garden displays the character of untamed nature in distinct contrast to the hard edges of the urban context. Vines and trees that respond to sun exposure and wind direction are particularly effective in evoking a picturesque aura.

No space is too small to insert a landscape. Here is an opportunity to create a miniature world of natural beauty punctuated with sculpture and framed by an artistic backdrop.

39

On a large roof, consider a low-maintenance landscape that needs only minimal soil depth to support indigenous plants. Bold swaths of texture and color create seasonally changing patterns that are a delight from upper apartments as well as adjacent terraces.

Green roofs are becoming increasingly popular. Developed as a means to mitigate some of the ill effects of the urban environment, low-maintenance planted roofs are both beautiful and functional.

42

The perimeter of a sky garden must be safe as well as attractive. If the existing edge is too low, vertical extenders can be added. This terrace uses a wall-mounted attachment to avoid replacing the terra cotta coping.

Railings, Fences, and Screens

By twisting flat stainless steel rails, a distinctive pattern is created when raked by sunlight.

Perforated stainless steel panels provide a non-climbable enclosure yet allow a filtered view beyond.

Taller security or privacy fences can be made less imposing by welding playful figures on to the painted vertical louvers. *Photo by Max Donoso Saint.*

The traditional craft of wrought iron using a floral motif adds detail and texture to the garden's boundary.

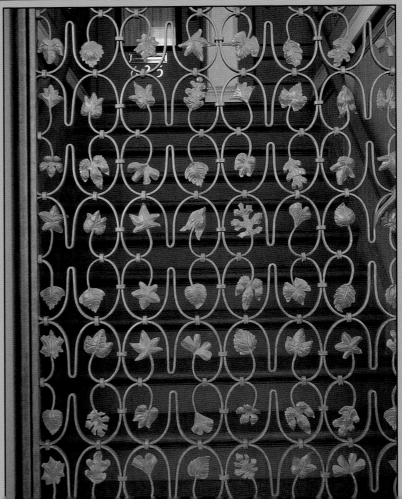

A simple painted wood railing is harmonious with the architecture and its waterfront location. Local building codes govern overall railing height and spacing of vertical pickets.

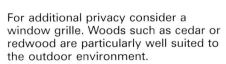

For additional privacy consider a window grille. Woods such as cedar or redwood are particularly well suited to the outdoor environment.

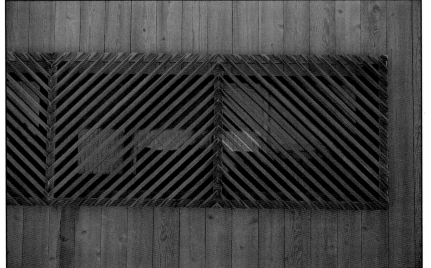

45

Gates signify a passage from one place to another. This whimsical painted wood gate is as much sculptural as it is functional.

46

A unique three dimensional effect is created by columns made from staggered bricks. The pattern permits cooling breezes to pass through while affording visual privacy.

Inexpensive and durable, a wood stockade fence can be readily attached to a railing. Be sure to have an engineer verify if your existing conditions are strong enough to withstand the added wind load of a solid enclosure.

Vertical boards set in a staggered pattern offer the advantage that both sides of the fence are equally attractive to you and your neighbors.

47

Horizontally set boards of two sizes create a subtle pattern and lower the sense of height. Intentional gaps between the boards reduce wind resistance. *Photo by Max Donoso Saint.*

Opposing page:
Bamboo is strong and rot resistant. Using traditional rope fasteners, this frame supports a reed screen creating a distinctively Asian setting.

49

50

By combining the strength of a metal frame with dense wood lattice panels, a tall privacy screen is achieved. The white color makes this fence a more prominent visual feature while a dark color would make it recede.

Roofs often contain noisy or unappealing mechanical equipment. A solid folded metal panel masks an air conditioning unit and provides a foil for a dwarf magnolia tree.

Lattice panels affixed to the wall create a classical garden feel. The tromp l'oeil design creates the illusion of depth on the wall surface.

51

Pre-fabricated wood lattice panels are used to define this outdoor room. The lower wall-mounted section contains the standard diamond shaped spacing while the upper section has removed every other slat to create a less dominant covering. The perpendicular divider is made by doubling the panels to produce greater visual separation.

A trellis fence between two terraces affords both privacy and a frame for a desirable view beyond. This sitting spot is strategically located to take advantage of the opening.

Progressively spaced wood members provide privacy where it is needed and dissolve into an airy vine support at its upper reaches.

A lightweight galvanized steel sandwich welcomes vines to weave through its framework letting the plants do the work of screening.

Impinging on a neighbor's brick wall is avoided by constructing a free-standing metal trellis. Use twining rather than clinging vines to ensure the foliage stays on your side of the property.

In a very narrow space, a contemporary trellis of aluminum frame and steel cable infill creates a luxuriant green mural.

54

Cooling breezes and a filtered view are made possible with this green screen of generously spaced steel cables. Seasonal clipping is required to maintain the openings between the grid.

Arbors and Sun Shades

A free-standing arbor defines a special place within a large sky garden. This structure establishes a sheltered destination within the outdoor room and forms a welcoming space within which to cluster seating.

56

Constructing an arbor may require a professional to engineer the support system. An adjacent wall can help to anchor the beams; waterproofed pitch pockets or ground sleeves hold the posts to the roof slab. Additional stability is provided with integrally attached benches.

An arbor may be used to define a passage from one part of a terrace to another. Supported by planters and smothered with vines, this hallway has a compressed feeling and beckons the visitor to seek the bench at the end of the corridor.

59

This arbor of teak beams and tubular bronze rods relies on the dead weight of a planter for its support. The elegantly understated structure is also proportioned for the growth habit of grape vines that emerge from the anchoring container.

60

Expensive arbors can be substituted with a simple metal mesh. Select the mesh dimension that best suits the vine specie that will do the work of shading the space below.

Even if your terrace lacks an appealing vista, a small arbor inset creates a frame in which to make your own intimate view of a special garden ornament.

The combination of robust elements effectively forms a dynamic space with year round shade and privacy.

61

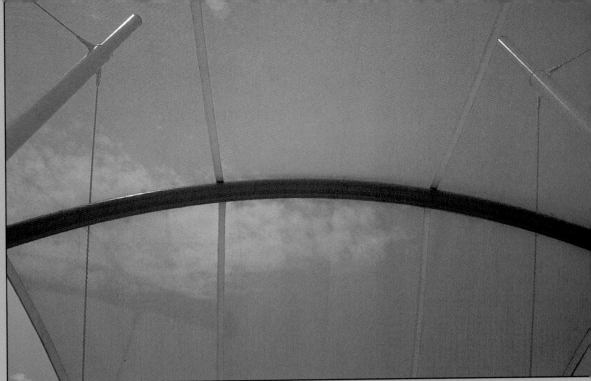

There are a variety of vinyl and polyester fabrics available that can be attached to supports to offer filtered shade. Be sure to use a mesh type fabric to allow rain to pass through or construct the frame with a pitch to shed water.

Wrought iron panels are used to fabricate a total enclosure complete with bench and air conditioner cover that turns this narrow passage into a gardenesque corridor.

62

A retractable canvas awning is adaptable in climates where the need for sun control varies with the seasons. More advanced mechanical systems are fitted with sensors that automatically retract the awning when wind speed reaches a level that might pose a hazard.

63

64

Wood decking constructed in modular sizes is easy to install and provides a level surface even if the roof is uneven. Decking units allow for free passage of water and can be picked up to clean drains below.

A Palette of Materials

The floor of a sky garden plays a critical role in its aesthetic character. Paving establishes a sense of movement, creates spatial relationships, and organizes plantings and furnishings. Large paving units tend to make an area feel less spacious while smaller pavers make a space feel bigger. Selection of appropriate surface materials is governed by the existing roof condition, drainage pattern, your budget, and the garden's style.

Rotation of modular decking units creates a checkerboard pattern that breaks up the expanse of wood.

Opposing page:
Introducing a diagonal pattern reinforces a special vantage point on the terrace. The consistent use of wood for the floor, planters, and fence ties the design elements together.

Elevating the deck above the roof surface allows planters to be recessed accentuating the feeling of an unbroken expanse.

Precast concrete pavers may be set directly on a roof surface or raised on pedestals. A wide range of colors and textures is available from which to create patterns. Strong accent colors within the field of paving direct the viewer's attention to a special feature or vista.

Smaller precast concrete pavers are more suited to making intricate patterns such as a herringbone style.

A pedestal system elevates the paver above the roof surface allowing unimpeded flow of water and occasional roof inspections. Pedestals may be used with a variety of pavers including precast concrete and stone. Smaller pebbles may be used along irregular edges to avoid expensive cutting.

Stone pavers can be set directly onto a roof surface. This non-directional slate pattern also incorporates the subtle color variations available in many stone types.

Bluestone pavers in two sizes offer the ability to define smaller spaces within a larger field of paving. Select a thermal or split-face finish to avoid slippery conditions.

Granite is one of the more expensive stone paving materials but it is extremely durable and is available in a wide range of colors. Mixing subdued colors in a non-directional pattern mitigates large expanses of dull paving.

69

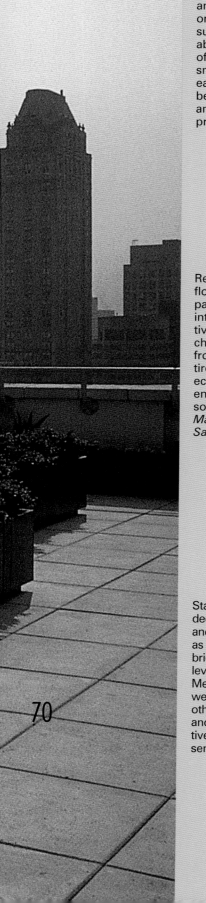

High density plastic mats are an economical solution to cover an unattractive or rough roof surface. Available in a range of colors, they snap together easily and may be cut to fit odd angles or protrusions.

Resilient rubber flooring converts part of this roof into an imaginative play area for children. Made from recycled tires, it is both economical and environmentally sound. *Photo by Max Donoso Saint.*

Stainless steel decking is strong and can be used as steps or a bridge to span level changes. Metal combines well with many other materials and has a distinctive modern sensibility.

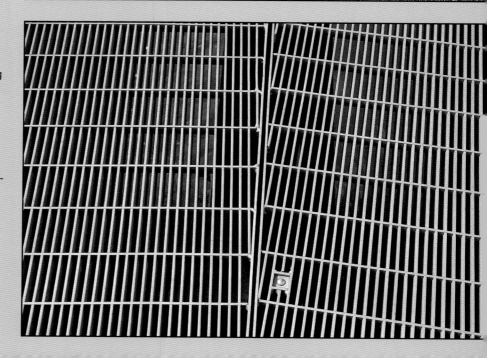

Not all of the floor needs to be covered with walkable materials. By combining industrial fiberglass decking units with volcanic pebbles, the ultimate in lightweight surfacing is achieved.

One of the most common surfaces is quarry tile. Selection of fired clay or glazed tiles is determined by your climate but the pattern and colors should be chosen to complement the architecture and terrace design.

71

Bluestone and Mexican beach pebbles are arranged to create a pattern that is coordinated with recessed planting beds and garden access. *Photo by Max Donoso Saint.*

Shallow modular containers hold moss and glossy black pebbles on this shady terrace. The checkerboard is interrupted by a dry streambed of unpolished river stones. *Photo by Max Donoso Saint.*

The terrace floor is an ideal surface on which to set an artistic element. A sand cast concrete paver with a botanical motif draws the eye downward and enlivens an otherwise ordinary field of paving.

Variation in level, reinforced by a change in paving materials and judiciously placed planters, establishes two distinct spaces - one for sitting and one for walking.

Large roof areas benefit from even a modest change in level. The two-step platform of recycled timber creates a separate area for informal lounging. *Photo by Max Donoso Saint.*

73

What better way to herald an alfresco entertaining area than by adding a dance floor. Low planters define the entrance and boundaries of this multi-purpose outdoor surface.

A raised deck at the end of the terrace takes advantage of higher perimeter walls and offers a quiet, protected refuge.

76

Above & opposing page:
Containers are a necessity in sky gardens. There is a limitless array of shapes, sizes, and materials to suit your imagination. They can be foreground or background objects, a collectible, or a recycled item. Smaller pots and urns can be relocated seasonally to create new compositions of color or accent features. Selection of the right container depends on many factors including the garden style, planting design, climate, weight, and budget.

Pots and Urns

Small containers such as a glazed terra cotta urn are well suited to simple planting such as a sculptural cactus. Situated by the gate, it heralds the garden style within.

78

Some planters are sculptures themselves. The floral headdress of a Mexican figurine can be changed seasonally but such a shallow dish needs daily watering to keep plants thriving.

This amusing double-headed creature is served well by a pair of pineapple plants. Reinvigorate your décor by moving small planters to new locations.

The very visible front of a planter may be a surface on which to display ornamentation as is done here with a cast iron relief. Topiary evergreens and floral accents echo the container's traditional style.

Everyday objects can be recycled to take on a new role as a container. A banded oak barrel fits comfortably in a 19th century brick setting.

A cottage garden is evoked by the wooden wheelbarrow quaintly planted with daylilies. Placed diagonally, it helps resolve an awkward corner.

An old amphora, though patched and painted, is picturesque when filled with intensely red geraniums.

Terra cotta with its warm coloration and varied styles makes a versatile container. Its portability allows for seasonal rearrangement to create new combinations of grouped plantings.

Cast stone describes a type of concrete that can be molded into many shapes. Elegant and formal, this container adds a charming traditional touch to the garden.

82

Painted metal cubes are lightweight and can be grouped together to form the appearance of a continuous planter.

These unpainted galvanized metal cylinders can be moved about the terrace to set up a rhythmic pattern along the stucco wall or clustered to form an herb garden outside the kitchen door.

Architectural refinement is evident in this well proportioned ledge planter. The glossy black finish is a perfect foil against which to display colorful flowers and small leafed foliage.

Large Containers

Wood is a popular choice for large planters. The decorative inset and white color lend elegance. Light colored planters effectively show off foliage and bright flowers.

Opposing page:
A two-toned simple wood container blends harmoniously with the architectural features. The bold form of dark green holly shrubs complements the understated composition.

It is important to select a container size that is consistent with the soil volume demand of the plants. Trees will only thrive in commensurately large planters. Know your roof's weight load capacity before starting a planting design. *Photo by James Morse*.

Wood containers will last longer if their corners are reinforced with metal. These redwood planters with copper corners are also lined with galvanized sheet metal to add further protection against rot.

To create a neutral background against which to display plants, these cedar-faced planters have been stained with preservative bleaching oil to give them a gray beige cast.

Elevated planters are prominently visible and need to be well constructed. Simple detailing of the planter and trellis band creates an graceful linear motif along the terrace wall.

87

Custom made containers have the advantage of solving technical problems. This wood planter has been constructed around protruding vent pipes that disappear behind a group of tall evergreen shrubs.

A two-tiered planter arrangement uses the plants of the lower container to mask the taller one. When filled with billowing roses and cascading evergreens the effect is strikingly lush.

A look inside and under a wood planter reveals some of the keys to successful container construction. The planter bottom has ample drainage holes that are then covered with a layer of lightweight volcanic gravel to encourage water movement. The filter mat prevents soil from escaping and staining the floor. Styrofoam insulation lines the planter sides to protect roots from sudden temperature fluctuations and keeps moisture from constant contact with the wood. To facilitate moving the large planter for roof inspections or to create new container arrangements, heavy-duty casters are secured to the planter base.

Lightweight concrete is a durable and attractive alternative to wood containers. Simple shapes make them fine choices for modern terraces. Using planters of different heights can increase the perceived distance of a space.

Many color and texture options are available in lightweight concrete planters. Similar earth tones in the pavers, furnishings, and planter are contrasted with the bamboo planting. *Photo by Max Donoso Saint.*

90

Fiberglass, the lightest of all container materials, is available in custom or standard sizes. Pebbled or sandblasted finishes have a more natural look than the glossy finish of typical fiberglass. *Photo by Max Donoso Saint.*

An ordinary container can be covered in a special material to make it a center piece. The minimalist plantings and forms of the terrace perimeter set off the bronze clad planter with its pendulous branched tree.

Metals for use as planter material need to be chosen for rust resistance as well as appearance. Galvanized steel is treated with a protective coating and, shown here with its grade marking, is the ultimate in a contemporary industrial style.

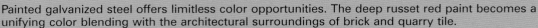

Painted galvanized steel offers limitless color opportunities. The deep russet red paint becomes a unifying color blending with the architectural surroundings of brick and quarry tile.

92

Galvanized sheet metal has the advantage of being easily fabricated in curved forms. The concave shape is accentuated by cascading evergreens that frame delicate annuals. The convex shape is placed opposite a door to provide greater planting width for an evergreen tree that becomes the focal point of an indoor outdoor relationship.

This arrangement of sheet metal containers and their plant selection has been coordinated with the terrace boundary. The larger container plays up the rhythm of masonry piers and is filled with a shrub appropriately proportioned to the architecture and dramatic views.

94

Opposing page:
Industrial diamond-plate sheets can be fabricated into serviceable containers and create an interesting modern look when juxtaposed with a low boxed hedge and small round tree.

Photo by Max Donoso Saint.

Plants transform the sky garden and give your sanctuary character, seasonal pleasure, and distinctive beauty. There are endless ways to combine colors, textures, and shapes that can focus the viewer's attention or withdraw into the background.

Creating a Framework

Photo by James Morse.

Punctuating a linear arrangement of planters with trees is an effective means to create a rhythm and break up a monotonous line. Trees require the greatest amount of soil volume so careful selection of species is critical. Needle evergreens such as atlas cedar *(Cedrus atlantica)* with its airy branching habit, is a fine choice for its tolerance to wind.

Evergreen trees and shrubs, all of the juniper *(Juniperus)* family establish the vertical accents in terra cotta planters, screen the perimeter railing, and cascade over the planter face. This combination provides a year-round framework among which seasonal flowers provide colorful contrast.

Alternating needle and broadleaf evergreens carve out pockets for annuals and create texture and color diversity in all seasons.

99

Needle evergreen trees such as pine *(Pinus)* and juniper *(Juniperus)* create a dense and lush background against which to place contrasting forms and colors. *Photo by James Morse.*

Consider the tones of your surroundings. Dark green false cypress *(Chamaecyparis)*, cascading junipers, and bright flowers are highlighted by the light brick wall, pavers, and beige planter.

A clipped privet *(Ligustrum)* hedge forms an architectural green foil to a colorful annual plant association.

A mixture of broadleaf evergreens establishes a strong line of foliage that corresponds to the railing height. A larger curved planter provides additional space for a tiered evergreen combination of Japanese garden juniper *(Juniperus procumbens)*, andromeda *(Pieris)* and Hollywood juniper *(Juniperus torulosa)*.

For a complete privacy screen, tightly spaced Sky Rocket juniper *(Juniperus chinensis 'Sky Rocket')* terminate the terrace and offer a blue-green backdrop for textured foreground plantings.

More simple and bold is this clipped hedge of Egyptian star cluster *(Pentas lanceolata)* that corresponds to the horizontal line of the perimeter wall. Its dense red flower clusters are prominent throughout the summer and autumn in warm climates.

Framework plants may also recede into the background so that seasonally striking plants such as Hortensia hydrangea *(Hydrangea macrophylla)*, colorful annuals, and perennials are allowed to shine.

A common characteristic of a terrace or balcony is its linearity. Take advantage of this by using a neutral evergreen shrub such as inkberry *(Ilex glabra)* to form a backdrop against which to display accents of visual interest with seasonal flowers.

In wider planters arrange plants in layers, creating a foreground, midground and background. Large leafed plantain lily *(Hosta)* serves as a filler between the taller and shorter mixed border plants.

Planting in Small Containers

Urns and pots offer special opportunities and limitations in planting design. It is most important to coordinate the container size and its style with appropriately scaled plants. This Italianate terra cotta pot is proportionately suited to a large evergreen shrub.

Urns can be living flower arrangements. A mono-chromatic planting of upright and cascading plants relies on textures and leaf colors for its captivating appearance.

This simple square terra cotta container is perfectly sized for a topiary fuchsia under-planted with ivy.

105

106

Annual potato vine *(Ipomoea)* completely obscures the container. Fragrant heliotrope *(Heliotropium)* and ornamental grasses *(Pennisetum)* complete the living arrangement. *Photo by Max Donoso Saint.*

When selecting plants for small containers, consider the vantage point from which they will be seen. A window box is visible from inside as well as from below so the choice of upright and cascading plants is appropriate.

This planter is viewed at eye level where the combination of ornamental grasses and delicate flowers is best appreciated.

This planter is viewed from above where cushion-like plantings of petunias and heliotrope nestle among a variety of low evergreen shrubs.

107

Living Sculpture

Few families of plants are as innately sculptural as the cactus. When given ample room around each plant and set against a simple earth-toned backdrop, individual species become an animate gallery of forms.

Clipped or topiary shrubs such as oleander *(Nerium)* are also sculptural. Bold forms are powerful objects and should be granted ample breathing room to be seen as a specimen or featured plant.

Combining a two dimensional wall painting with three dimensional plants blurs reality and artifice to create illusionary magic in a narrow space.

Even in an extremely narrow space, a wall surface can be transformed into architectural sculpture. Variegated Algerian ivy *(Hedera colchica dentata 'Variegata')* has been meticulously pruned along a grid of cables to create a sculpture in relief.

109

This spiral juniper is an example of the traditional art of topiary. Its distinct formality needs high maintenance and is best placed at a threshold or other prominent location.

A dramatic arrange-ment of cut tree trunks and birch branches achieves the ultimate in low maintenance natural sculpture.

110

Plant Combinations

Good planting design is based on arranging textures, colors, and shapes in a way that suits your taste and needs. After you have determined the framework and sculptural accents, the next step is to consider forms and textures.

Textures can be subtly integrated using only delicate shades of green. This shade garden relies on a low ground cover combination of ferns, periwinkle, and sweet woodruff for its effect.

This grouping combines the variegated spiky foliage of gold sword yucca *(Yucca filamentosa)* with a round red-leafed barberry *(Berberis thunbergii atropurpurea)*. Placed in the foreground, these contrasting textures and colors become dominant.

Repetition of plant form is another way to reinforce texture. Grassy upright foliage fills the background while more transparent spires of muted colors imbue an untamed feeling.

Contrasting flower forms is a seasonal example of a way to create textural interest. The strong umbel-shaped flowers of ice plant *(Sedum 'Autumn Joy')* are set off with an under planting of delicate wormwood *(Artemisia)*.

Spikes of annual purple salvia *(Salvia sclarea)* are interplanted with bell-shaped tobacco flower *(Nicotiana)*. Equally tall and of similar color intensity, the flower form combination is captivating.

Soft spires of pink phlox *(Phlox paniculata)* are paired with round headed globe thistle *(Echinops)* to create a midground punctuation amid a grouping of shrubs.

114

A dense backdrop of shrubs blocks the wind allowing button head and daisy petalled pink perennials to display their individual personalities.

Color Combinations

A monochromatic planting uses shades, tints, and tones of a single hue. The restrained composition of grays and greens illustrates the effectiveness of plant forms to create a soothing picture of striking visual interest.

Harmonious color combinations use two to three colors that are adjacent to each other on the color wheel such as yellow, orange, and red. A warm palette of colors tends to appear closer to the viewer because of its intensity.

The addition of white and gray flowers and foliage softens the high contrast of the deep yellows and oranges.

This riot of reds, pinks, and salmons illustrates the powerful effect of hot colors to envelop a tiny terrace. Stark contrasts and vivid colors are best suited to strong sunlight.

119

Misty shades of lavender and gray garden verbena *(Verbena)* unite the light colored architectural features and black tile floor.

Below:
Deep purple umbels of heliotrope gracefully combine with spires of purple and white angelonia *(Angelonia)*. Bold gray foliage eases the transition between the contrasting colors and forms.

120

Complementary colors are contrasting hues and lie opposite each other on the color wheel. One of the most pleasing combinations is yellow and purple created here with heliotrope and Dahlberg daisy *(Dyssodia tenuiloba)*.

This complementary color scheme uses a greater diversity of shades in the yellow and purple family. Ample space is allotted to green foliage to avoid visual chaos.

121

A similar device is to use gray foliage plants like wormwood and catmint *(Nepeta)* to subdue strong contrasting colors.

Red and green are complementary colors. Small red flowers and foliage are balanced by bold lime green plantain lily *(Hosta)* leaves.

Triads are groups of three colors that are equidistant from each other on the color wheel. Without trying these colors together, you might never imagine purple, pink, and russet as a fetching combination. The gray foliage and container color help unite the composition.

The key to any color combination is repetition. The red dahlias of the background are repeated as red shrub foliage in the foreground while the whites and grays form a soothing midground.

123

Seasonal Change

In northern climates seasonal transitions are often marked by the appearance of flowers or leaf color change. A sourwood *(Oxydendron arboreum)* shown in spring and fall illustrates the importance of selecting plants that have multiple seasons of interest when a sky garden has limited planting space.

In southern arid climates the cactus offers striking form and dramatic colors for year round effect.

As winter turns to spring, squill *(Scilla siberica)* peeking up through the melting snow is a welcome sight.

125

A mass of pastel colored tulips glistering in the morning sun is a sure sign that spring has arrived.

Even in a small planter primary colors of spring bulbs make a captivating arrangement.

As spring turns to summer the dried flower stalks of globular giant onion (*Allium giganteum*) add a textural note of seasonal transition.

Hot colors of this summer flower border last until the first frost.

The pendulous yellow blooms of a golden chain tree *(Laburnum)* are harbingers of summer.

The native fragrant beach rose *(Rosa rugosa)* displays the onset of autumn when its rosehips appear alongside continuing blooms.

In autumn, a golden cast envelopes a cut-leaf Japanese maple *(Acer palmatum dissectum)* in stark contrast to the evergreen junipers.

Autumn is the best season for ornamental grasses when their fox-tail seed heads arching over slender stems glisten in the early afternoon.

Spent summer annuals can be replaced with autumn-
flowering chrysanthemums. Seasonal replanting is a necessity for maximum floral display in narrow planters.

Right & top right:
Shrubs and vines reveal brilliant
deep colors in autumn. Even
broadleaf evergreens like azalea
(Azalea hino-crimson) is tinged
with maroon after the first frost.
Virginia creeper *(Parthenocissus
quinquefolia)* begins to set fruit as
its leaves turn crimson.

Many members of the holly *(Ilex)* family produce bright red berries among their broadleaf evergreen foliage as an indication of winter.

In winter, a narrow planter is filled with cut branches of pine, cedar, and winterberry to avoid the dreary look of an empty container.

A sunny, exposed sky garden has similar climatic characteristics as a shoreline: strong winds, intense sun, and periods of drought. Plants that naturally grow in these conditions such as pines and beach rose are well adapted to rooftops.

Prevailing winds can permanently alter the growth habit of a tree. Members of the juniper family withstand strong wind and can even take on a sculptural form as a result.

131

More protected locations offer greater options for tree types. Paperbark maple *(Acer griseum)* can take shade as well as full sun when sheltered from strong wind.

Shrubs are the workhorses of the terrace garden. Unlike trees, they are sure to stay in bounds of the available space. Shrubs can be grouped to form pleasing combinations of color, shape, and texture.

A specimen is a plant whose characteristics and placement give it prominence. A golden mop *(Chamaecyparis pisifera)* is positioned strategically at a visible corner where it can be appreciated standing alone.

Roses of all kinds do remarkably well in sky gardens. They are seldom attacked by the diseases and pests that plague roses in damp enclosed in-ground gardens.

133

134

Butterfly bush *(Buddleia)* lives up to its name. It is equally attractive to humans who can enjoy its long bloom time and delicate arching habit.

Cascading shrubs are vital to the container garden as their pendulous branches soften planter walls. Cotoneaster *(Cotoneaster adpressus praecox)* has the added pleasure of tiny white flowers and bright red berries.

Vines have a special place in sky gardens where they can scramble up an arbor and provide both welcome shade and color. Trumpet vine *(Campsis radicans)* is a rapid grower and will twine around a post.

135

What could be more romantic than sitting under an arbor where bunches of delicious grapes *(Vitis)* are suspended above you.

Vines can imbue a protected terrace with fragrance. Gold flame honeysuckle *(Lonicera heckrottii)* is a free flowering variety that is both sweet smelling and colorful.

136

The soft summer afternoon sun backlights deep red bougainvillea *(Bougainvillea)* bracts engulfing a fence.

137

For a year-round effect, try combining vines. Here wintercreeper *(Euonymous fortunei)* clings to the wall and shows off the seasonal glory of old man's beard *(Clematis)*.

Boston ivy *(Parthenocissus tricuspidata)* spreads its clinging tendrils and turns a dull façade into a green wall. In autumn this will turn a blaze of fiery red.

138

Left & above:
Bamboo, often considered a pest in courtyard gardens, is a fine choice in containerized sky gardens where its aggressive spreading habit is kept in check. There are bamboo varieties to suit most climates and offer great diversity in culm coloration and growth habit.

139

Left & below left:
Ornamental grasses are well suited to windy sun-swept terraces where their fountain-like foliage and plumes respond to the slightest breeze. Place them where the sun will highlight their leaf coloration and flower heads.

Ground cover is the name given to a wide variety of plants whose purpose is to fill in the spaces between the taller shrubs or flowers. They may be combined or planted as a mass of a single specie.

Hakone grass *(Hakonechloa macra 'Aureola')* massed as a solid ground cover has distinctive variegated golden foliage that brightens even a shady area.

Bearberry *(Arcostaphylos uva-ursi)* is a versatile four-season ground cover. In addition to the pale pink spring flowers, it produces bright red berries in summer and its evergreen foliage turns bronze-purple in winter.

142

Perennials come back every year. Selection of these flowering plants needs to be made wisely as they can consume precious space in the limited container garden. Species such as African lily *(Agapanthus)* are an excellent choice in warmer climates because of their long summer bloom and attractive foliage.

Red ginger *(Alpinia)* and bird of paradise *(Strelitzia)* are bold and striking. Their flower shapes, colors, and foliage make them dramatic choices for warm climates.

143

144

The papery petals of oriental poppy *(Papaver orientalis)* appear fragile but are remarkably tolerant of heat on a sun filled terrace. An interesting feature is the appearance of both the buds and seed pods before and after bloom.

Plantain lily *(Hosta)* is a mainstay of shady gardens. Available in almost limitless varieties, they are selected primarily for their foliage effect.

The muted color of lavender *(Lavandula)* belies its delicious fragrance and year-round effect. Collect flower heads to dry for indoor arrangements and potpourris.

145

For a native garden, late blooming coneflower *(Echinacea)* and joe pye weed *(Eupatorium)* are a reliable choice and do not need the coddling of exotic species. You may soon find butterflies fluttering among the flowers as they are attracted to these perennials.

146

Most annuals such as these marigolds *(Tagetes)* come in a variety of colors and sizes so check the labels before buying them out of bloom.

Annuals have particular merit in a sky garden. When planting space is limited, annuals can be replaced seasonally for constant bloom and allow you to change the color scheme every year.

Sometimes color variation is of no concern especially when massing the same type of plant, as with these shade-tolerant impatiens.

Tobacco plant comes in many heights and colors. The taller variety is pleasantly fragrant at night while the shorter varieties offer non-stop blooms throughout the summer.

148

Spring isn't the only season for bulbs. Dahlias *(Dahlia)* and tiger lilies *(Lilium)* are bulbs too. Their long bloom period and intense fragrance make them a good choice for a cutting garden.

149

Your sky garden offers the opportunity to linger outdoors in solitude or with friends. Locating places to read, dine, or relax needs to be considered in relation to the ambience you wish to create. Comfort, views, shade, and intimacy are qualities that foster prolonged enjoyment.

Chapter Six

Furnishing the Outdoors

Portable Furniture

The ornate metalwork of the high backed chairs recalls the Victorian era. These fanciful pieces are best used for décor rather than comfortable lounging.

A painted metal love seat is nestled in a corner with its back to the world. Dark green foliage sets off the white furniture and is an inviting view even when not in use.

An Adirondack chair and side table create a cozy nook when protected from wind by a trained shrub espaliered on a trellis.

Wire grid furniture is well suited to wet climates where rain will not collect on the surfaces. Their openness offers no wind resistance so there is no concern that the furniture might blow off the terrace.

An eclectic mix of furniture styles forms a pleasing arrangement when set among a neutral envelope of planting.

153

Formal low planting beds frame a teak bench to create a focal point. Teak is an excellent, rot resistant wood that absorbs neither heat nor cold making it comfortable in any location. *Photo by Max Donoso Saint.*

A woven wicker loveseat placed in dappled shade with its back to the world, beckons an intimate pause. Protective coatings ensure comfort and longevity of the materials.

Furniture can be used as a sculptural object. A cast stone bench with ornate supports complements the formal garden style.

Each element on this modern terrace is striking, yet by using simple shapes many materials can be combined in one space. The lounge chairs and dining settees are cast aluminum; the tabletop is a composite stone.

On a protected roof wind is not a concern allowing the use of comfortable and light-weight aluminum and vinyl mesh chairs. Neutral colors are harmonious with the modern architecture.

155

Consider your entertaining style when selecting and arranging furniture. For evening cocktails and buffet style dining this grouping of a love seat, two chairs, and a long low table is a perfect invitation. *Photo by Max Donoso Saint.*

If the terrace is your private sanctuary, a single chair, small table, and lounge chair will suffice. Place the furniture to take advantage of a dramatic view or to create your own view with profuse plantings.

A long terrace with expansive views needs plant groupings to create more intimate spaces in which to place a dining area. The stone bench doubles as a sideboard and a glass tabletop has the added feature of reflecting the pleasant surroundings.

157

A few stairs accentuated by a casual arrangement of geranium-filled pots beckons a visitor to the dining area. Creating separate outdoor rooms by level changes or plant groupings expands the usefulness of your terrace.

158

In hot climates or on a south facing terrace table umbrellas will make a midday meal more pleasant. Folding canvas umbrellas are a versatile choice so they can be closed on windy or cloudy days. *Photo by Max Donoso Saint.*

Metal furniture is often more comfortable when fitted with cushions. Coordinate colors with other related elements such as canvas awnings. A solid color rather than a pattern will work better with a rich plant palette.

Built-in Seating

These built-in love seats are arranged so portable tables can be brought to them. Hosting a large party is easily accommodated without the clutter of chairs.

A built-in bench in a corner performs a dual role to open up a spectacular view and to form a social gathering spot. The proportions allow for multiple uses from reclining to sitting or casual style dining. This idea is not recommended if you have small children who could climb up on the bench adjacent to the railing.

Roofs are full of objects that pop up through them. Skylights can be a hazard to a guest so this terrace has a bench around its perimeter. Simply designed, it offers casual sitting or sunbathing without obstructing views.

A discreet series of cylinders uplight the slender bamboo canes thrusting shadows against a light colored wall surface. During the day the black fixtures virtually disappear in the black stone mulch. *Photo by Max Donoso Saint.*

Artificial Light: Fixtures and Effects

Night lighting can dramatically change the mood and usefulness of a sky garden. Lights are best placed where they can highlight special features such as a fountain or sculptural tree or where they can encourage lingering in soft glowing light.

A single spot light skims the wall behind a special tree to accentuate its presence.
Photo by James Morse.

Small cylinders fitted with stakes allow easy adjustment of both location and angle of light. By placing two fixtures in opposite corners of the weeping elm tree, its form is evenly uplit. As the tree matures the fixtures can be redirected.

Bottom left & below:
Placement of spotlights is critical to the desired effect. This fixture has a hood to direct its beam at the sculpture and shields the viewer's eye from unwanted glare. Lights generate heat so plants need to be kept low or at some distance from the fixture to avoid scorching the foliage.

A diffused beam from a flood light is capable of illuminating a substantial area such as the canopy of a significant tree. Plants with medium to large leaves are better suited than needle evergreens to uplighting.

Adjustable wall mounted fixtures throw light on evergreen shrubs across a narrow terrace and are positioned to avoid shining into interior rooms.

Wall mounted copper down lights provide a soft ambient glow or overall illumination that is enhanced by the white surface. Uplights accentuate the large trees making their canopy visible at night.

For general illumination, surface mounted fixtures should be positioned to cast an even glow. Low wattage bulbs are recommended when the light source is visible.

A wall mounted copper coach lamp is appropriate in this garden setting. Placed next to the terrace door it illuminates the threshold.

This cast iron fixture is a striking ornament and is an appropriate choice for a 19th century building. Clear glass is traditionally used in period fixtures so placing them higher on a wall ensures protection from glare of a bright bulb.

Prominent fixtures near doors or windows should be fitted with translucent glass to diffuse light and reduce glare that is emitted from a visible bulb.

Select fixtures that are compatible in size and material with your garden style. A weathered copper fixture with a hood throws light downward and illuminates a distinctive architectural feature.

Evenly spaced tulip-shaped down lights provide even illumination in a narrow passage and are complemented by the tall loose foliage of annual flowers. The white trellis backdrop helps to further brighten the corridor.

169

Above:
The same fixtures are painted black to appear as part of the railing. Only at night is their utility visible as they direct soft illumination over the sitting area.

Right:
An aluminum and glass path light can be adapted for use in a planter. The top shield ensures that light is cast over the plants and not in the viewer's eyes.

Below:
Shielded step lights can also be adapted to planters by mounting or embedding them in planter walls. Regular spacing provides even light distribution in the walking area.

An overhead structure such as an arbor, densely shrouded with vines, is an ideal support from which to suspend a fixture. Exposed low voltage wiring can be hidden in the arbor's structure.

Plants and lighting can be intertwined. Wrapping a topiary with strings of glitter lights expresses the sculptural form for a dramatic evening effect.

171

Natural Light: Shadows and Reflections

You need not wait until evening to enjoy the effects of light. Ornamental ironwork surrounding the terrace can create beautiful patterns on the terrace floor.

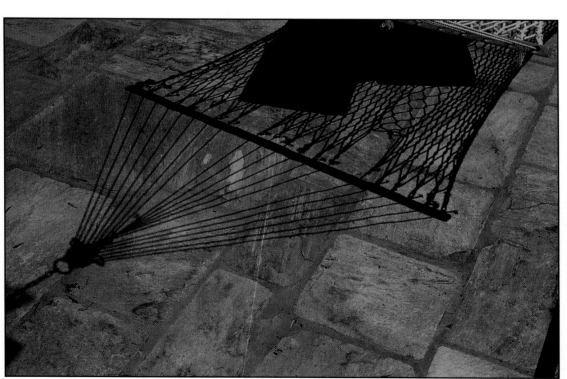

The shadow of a hammock with cushions projects the restfulness on to the ground.

Foliage patterns from a nearby grape vine enliven an otherwise dull wall.

The overhead bamboo shade structure casts its shadow on an adjacent wall continuing the pattern and extending its enveloping effect.

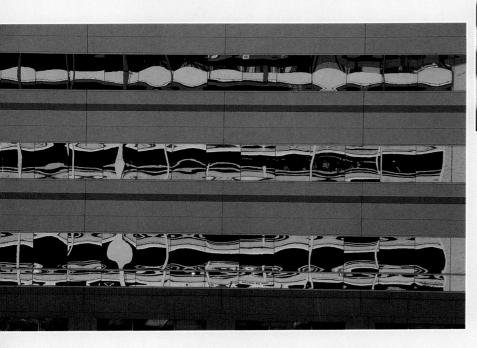

Innovations in glass making expand opportunities to use windows in modern buildings as dramatic reflective surfaces.

Before acquiring a piece of sculpture, look around at what your building has to offer. Details of the architecture can spark ideas on style and regional traditions. Brick buildings frequently use stone accents around windows and doors. Use these as cues for selecting appropriate ornaments such as a terra cotta pot grouping.

If a terrace can take the weight, there are many cast stone ornaments available on the market. This replica lends a distinctly classical accent to the garden.

Sculpture and Ornaments

A large sculpture should be a focal feature. To set it off, use a contrasting colored backdrop such as this dark copper and lattice bower. The figurative sculpture takes center stage when combined with a shallow zinc planter and low plants.

Situated to capture sunlight, this gilded figurine gleams brilliantly against a dark background. The statue's presence can be appreciated from indoors as well as while seated at the table.

A wading bird placed within an accordant planting evokes the water habitat of the sculpture. Its elegant lines are silhouetted against a copper and brass mesh screen.

A niche or ledge provides an ideal location to place objects. Even a modest recess converts utilitarian or found artifacts into a sculptural display.

Contemporary sculpture may be combined with a single specimen tree. The dramatic contrast of shapes and color changes character from day to night with the help of overhead lights that cast their shadows on the white wall.

Not all sculpture needs to be free-standing. Consider embedding a figurine or natural element into a wall for an edgy, high-impact effect.

177

More modest in scale but equally interesting is to set traditional glazed tiles into a stucco wall. Repeating the motif at various heights responds to the architectural enclosure and combines effectively with plantings.

Sculpture need not be an expensive or permanent investment. A wooden dough box holds mementos from a seashore vacation.

Mirrors may be set in a sculptural frame to visually enlarge a small space. The art deco mirror reflects a mass of colorful tulips that change seasonally with different arrangements of annuals.

Fencing that encloses part of a terrace or rooftop is the perfect location to add decorative elements. Welding a panel of painted motifs from nature transforms an ordinary urban scene into a visual delight.

180

Create your own sculptural effect by inserting a tromp l'oeil lattice design into a sealed up window. The illusion of greater depth is created when combined with tiered plantings.

Placed directly opposite a terrace door, the painting blurs spatial limits and adds the impression of another garden just beyond the wall. The tromp l'oeil is equally effective from the dining table where the painting's detail can be appreciated.

This tromp l'oeil painting transforms an emergency exit door. The painted vista adds depth and artistry to a visual dead end. The Mediterranean look is extended by white-washing the brick wall on each side of the door.

181

Fountains and Water Effects

The sound and movement of water lend a special touch to a sky garden, but they can also add considerable weight. To alleviate this drawback, use a lightweight container such as a glass fiber reinforced concrete basin. This basin size is proportionate to the amount of splash created by falling water so this effect is best used on a protected terrace where wind will not contribute to overspray. *Photo by Max Donoso Saint.*

Though this pool appears heavy it is actually very shallow and is filled with lightweight volcanic stones. The dark colors add the illusion of depth and the modest bubblers of water offer a soothing sound without creating spray.

A tranquil fountain acts as both sculpture and focal point for an enclosed space. The centrally placed Italianate cast stone basin is framed by cascading ivy and small trees to create a distinctly classical style.

A small still pool is made from an inexpensive black plastic liner surrounded by bluestone. Combinations of delicate foliage soften the stone edge and provide an intimate moment in the garden.

A free standing water basin with a low jet is just the right amount of sound for the nearby sitting area. With or without water the Roman replica enlivens the inviting nook.

Gently cascading water from a shell basin is audible throughout the terrace. A dark green lattice backdrop highlights the light colored cast stone fountain in any season.

184

The mythological cast stone creature emits a distinctly cooling and mysterious effect when engulfed by moisture-loving ferns.

By combining a fountain with plantings, this driftwood and copper wall-mounted feature is pleasing with or without water flowing.

Centered opposite a prominent window, a trellis-mounted fountain flanked by trained ivy topiaries invites enjoyment of the scene from inside or out.

A volcanic stone basin, lightweight and watertight, evokes an Asian mood.

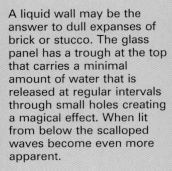

A liquid wall may be the answer to dull expanses of brick or stucco. The glass panel has a trough at the top that carries a minimal amount of water that is released at regular intervals through small holes creating a magical effect. When lit from below the scalloped waves become even more apparent.

To avoid problems with splashing water, try a fog fountain. Misters are placed within humidity-loving plants to produce an ethereal quality.

The sound of music can be especially enjoyable in a sky garden high above the noisy street. Custom made planters can be fitted with waterproof pockets in which to insert speakers. This semi-circular planter arrangement contains two speakers for balanced acoustics.

One would never suspect that this casually placed "rock" is actually a speaker. Interconnected by waterproof wiring, multiple speakers can be positioned throughout a terrace for uninterrupted listening pleasure. *Photo by James Morse.*

A waterproof shed is indispensable for storage of cushions, toys, or gardening supplies. Situated in a less prominent area of the terrace, this pre-fabricated aluminum enclosure provides ample capacity.

Left & Top left:
This wood planter houses a refrigerator. A magnetic spring lock and internal hinges disguise the door; a shallow metal pan at the top allows for sufficient soil depth to sustain annuals.

189

A wet bar is a great convenience on a terrace or roof where the kitchen may be remote from an outdoor entertaining area. Sinks with cold running water are easy to accommodate, as water is also needed for plantings. Stainless steel is an ideal material for basins and fixtures in the exterior environment.

Outdoor showers are not only for beach houses. Vertically set cedar planks with weathering oil preservative allow for a curved, rot-resistant privacy enclosure. A stainless steel showerhead is mounted to the building wall for direct connection to interior plumbing.

Using water vapor to lower temperatures in hot, dry climates is an ancient tradition. Contemporary irrigation systems may be fitted with small nozzles to emit a fine mist from an overhead structure to cool the environment below.

Awnings

Retractable Canvas Awnings
Avalon Garden—www.avalongarden.com
Euro Shutters—www.euroshutters.net
Retractable Awnings—www.retractableawnings.com
Screen Houses Limited—www.screen-house.com
Sunesta—www.sunesta.com

Enclosures: Arbors, Fencing, Lattice

Arbors: Cedar or Mahogany
Garden Structures—www.gardenstructure.com
Trellis Structures—www.trellisstructures.com

Arbors: Metal
G.I. Designs—www.gidesigns.net
Smith & Hawken—www.smithandhawken.com

Fencing: Bamboo Cane, Reed and Brushwood
Cherry Blossom Gardens—
www.cherryblossomgardens.com
Master Garden Products—www.mastergardenproducts.com
Palmyra Limited—www.bamboo-raffia.com

Fencing: Wood and Lattice Panels
Academy Fence—www.academyfence.com
Wayside Fence Company—www.waysidefence.com
Wood Classics—www.woodclassics.com

Flooring: Pavers and Decking

Stone Pavers
For distributors throughout the USA—
www.stonelocator.com

Glazed or Unglazed Tiles and Quarry Tiles
For distributors throughout the USA—
www.stonelocator.com
www.floorbiz.com

Precast Concrete Pavers
Davis Colors Paving Division—www.daviscolors.com
Hanover Pavers—www.hanoverpavers.com
RoofBlok Paver Systems—www.roofblok.com

Cedar Decking
For local retailers throughout USA—www.cedar-deck.org

Recycled Plastic Lumber Decking
For local retailers throughout USA—
www.epsplasticlumber.com

Rollout Wood Decking Mats
Mister Boardwalk—www.misterboardwalk.com

Fountains and Water Features

Container Fountains
A Birds World—www.abirdsworld.com
Christianne—www.christianne.com
Japanese Gifts—www.japanesegifts.com
J-Life International—www.jlifeinternational.com
Stonewear Fountains—www.stonewear.com

Wall-Mounted Fountains
Avalon Garden—www.avalongarden.com
Florentine Craftsmen—www.florentinecrafatsmen.com
Serenity Health—www.serenityhealth.com

Furniture

Teak Furniture
Atlantic Adirondack Chair & Furniture Company—
www.atlantic-adirondack.com
Barlow Tyrie—www.teak.com
Classic Teak—www.classicteak.com
Country Casual—www.countrycasual.com
Kingsley-Bate—www.kingsleybate.com
Tidewater Workshop—www.tidewaterworkshop.com
Wishing Well—www.mastergardenproducts.com

Wicker and Rattan Furniture
All American Pool and Patio—
www.allamericanpoolandpatio.com
Patio Life—www.patiolife.com
Porches and Yards—www.porchesandyards.com

Cast Aluminum and Wrought Iron Furniture
All American Pool and Patio—
www.allamericanpoolandpatio.com
Brown Jordan— www.brownjordan.com
Florence Craftsmen—www.florentinecraftsmen.com
Outdoor Classic Designs—www.outdoorclassicdesigns.com
Patio Life—www.patiolife.com
R.F. Coble Metal Design—www.coblemetalworks.com
Toscana Ceramics—www.toscanaceramics.com

Irrigation: Drip Systems for Container Plantings

Learn About Drip Irrigation
www.irrigationtutorial.com

Retail Manufacturers and Suppliers
Bowsmith Company—www.bowsmith.com
Dripworks—www.dripworksusa.com
Netafim USA—www.netafimusa.com
Submatic Irrigation Systems—www.submatic.com

Lighting: Low Voltage Outdoor

Deck, Step, and Hanging Lights
Kerr Lighting—www.kerrlighting.com
Landscape Lighting—www.usalight.com

Solar Lights
Creative Energy Technologies—www.cetsolar.com
Earth Forums—www.earthforums.com
Garden and Patio—www.garden-and-patio.com

Uplights
Cottage Outfitters—www.cottage-outfitters.com
Grand Light LLC—www.grandlight.com
Progress Lighting—www.nightsceneslighting.com
TerraDek—www.terradek.com
Vista Lighting—www.VistaPro.com

Ornaments

Lightweight Boulders and Faux Rocks
Planters by Design—www.plantersbydesign.com
Pond Biz—www.pondbiz.com
Rock and Water—www.rockandwater.com

Statuary
Architectural Pottery—www.archpot.com
Campania International —www.campaniainternational.com
Garden Planters—www.gardenplanters.com
Home and Vine Inc.—www.homeandvine.com
Kentucky American—www.kentuckyamerican.com
Stohans Gallery—www.stohans.com

Planters: Containers and Urns

Aluminum, Bronze, Copper Urns
Florida Plants—www.floridaplants.com
Gardécor—www.gardecor.com
Landplanfran—www.landplanfran.com

Cast Stone Urns
Architectural Pottery—www.archpot.com
Florida Plants—www.floridaplants.com
Haddonstone USA Limited—www.haddonstone.co.uk

Fiberglass and Plastic Pots and Planters
Architectural Precast—www.archprecast.com/plastic
Claycraft Planters—www.claycraft.com
Gainey Ceramics—www.gaineyceramics.com
Hummert International—www.hummert.com
Palmetto Planters—www.palmetto.com
Plant Containers—www.plantcontainers.com

Glazed Terra Cotta and Majolica Pots
Florida Plants—www.floridaplants.com
Garden Planters—www.gardenplanters.com
Gainey Ceramics—www.gaineyceramics.com

Lightweight Concrete Planters
Big Pots—www.bigpots.com
Dura Art Stone—www.duraartstone.com
Interlock Concrete Products, Inc.—www.ckweston.com/plant
Stonewear—www.stonewear.com

Self-Watering Plastic and Polyethelene Planters
Big Planters—www.bigplanters.com
Gardener's Supply Company—www.gardeners.com
Planter Technology—www.nsplants.com

Teak and Cedar Planters
Backyard Gardener—www.backyardgardener.com
Cottage Outfitters—www.cottage-outfitters.com
Master Garden Products—www.mastergardenproducts.com
Outdoor Abode—www.outdoorabode.com
Wishing Well—www.mastergardenproducts.com

Terra Cotta Pots and Urns
Arizona Pottery —www.arizonapottery.com
Campania International—www.campaniainternational.com
Garden Art International—www.gardenartint.com
Seibert and Rice—www.seibert-rice.com

Soil: Lightweight Planter Medium

Erth Products—www.erthproducts.com
Friendly Soil—www.escsi.org
Perma Till—www.permatill.com

Speakers for Outdoor Sound Systems

Speaker Manufacturers
A Brown Soun—www.abrown.com
Smart Home Products—www.smarthome.com
Stereo Speakers—www.stereospeakers.com

192